WEST COUNTRY COOK RECIPES

Elizabeth Hardy

DOMINO BOOKS (WALES) LTD

METRIC/IMPERIAL/AMERICAN UNITS

We are all used to doubling or halving a recipe. Thus, a Victoria sandwich may be made using 4 oz each of flour, sugar and butter with 2 eggs or 6 oz each of flour, sugar and butter with 3 eggs. The proportions of the ingredients are unchanged. This must be so for all units. Use either the metric units or the imperial units given in the recipes, do not mix the two.

It is not practical to give the exact equivalents of metric and imperial units because 1 oz equals 28.35 g and 1 pint equals 568 ml. The tables on page vi indicate suitable quantities but liquids should be carefully added to obtain the correct consistency. See also the charts on page iv.

PINTS TO MILLILITRES AND LITRES
The following are approximations only

¼ pint = 150 ml

½ pint = 275 ml

¾ pint = 425 ml

1 pint = 575 ml

1¾ pints = 1000 ml (1 litre)

3 pints = 1½ litres

CONTENTS

© D C P and E J P, 1993, 1994, 1996, 1997
Cover photograph by Jonathan Tew
Illustrations by Allison Fewtrell

ISBN 1 85772 054 7
Typeset by Domino Books (Wales) Ltd

The following charts give the approximate equivalents for metric and imperial weights, and oven temperatures.

Ounces	Approx g to nearest whole number	Approx g to nearest whole 25 g
1	28	25
2	57	50
3	85	75
4	113	125
5	142	150
6	170	175
7	198	200
8	226	225
9	255	250
10	283	275
11	311	300
12	340	350
13	368	375
14	396	400
15	428	425
16	456	450

OVEN TEMPERATURE GUIDE

	Electricity °C	°F	Gas Mark
Very cool	110	225	$\frac{1}{4}$
	130	250	$\frac{1}{2}$
Cool	140	275	1
	150	300	2
Moderate	170	325	3
	180	350	4
Moderately hot	190	375	5
	200	400	6
Hot	220	425	7
	230	450	8
Very hot	240	475	9

When using this chart for weights over 16 ounces, add the appropriate figures in the column giving the nearest whole number of grammes and then adjust to the nearest unit of 25. For example, 18 oz (16 oz + 2 oz) becomes 456 + 57 = 513 to the nearest whole number and 500 g to the nearest unit of 25.

Throughout the book, 1 teaspoon = 5 ml and 1 tablespoon = 15 ml.

FOREWORD

Traditional West Country cooking combines the essence of healthy eating with the rich produce from fertile farmland and pastures. Feasting has always been an important part of the farming calendar with lamb, beef and pork served with roasted apples, nuts and warm cakes washed down with heated ale and dry cider. Pigs fed on nuts and windfalls yield succulent meat and there is a long tradition of tasty pork pies and pasties in Wiltshire and Cornwall.

The apple orchards of Somerset have given us cider and it is hardly surprising that apples are the basis of many West Country recipes such as apple dumplings, Taunton Pudding with cider icing and Avalon Steam Pudding with an apple and suet base.

From earliest times, doughs and batters were cooked on a griddle. Today, brown eggs, rich milk, butter and cream are made into scones and cakes. Luscious soft fruits grow in abundance and the West Country is famous for its cream teas - strawberries, scones and fresh clotted cream.

World famous Cheddar cheese comes from this region. The rich pasturelands and mild climate produce a high milk yield which in turn produces the light yellow creamy texture and smooth taste characteristic of mature Cheddar. Stilton comes from this area too and so does the rich Blue Vinny of Dorset now at a premium in cheese circles.

With such a long coastline, seafood is part of the West Country's heritage. Pilchards, whiting, pollock and ling are used in restaurants throughout the region. Grilled mackerel stuffed with cream cheese, horseradish and onion and baked in dry cider is a typical recipe. But for a special occasion, there is Cornish crab pie: spiced brown crab with all the trimmings topped with clotted cream and covered with puff pastry.

Some of these recipes are in this book and others are in the two companion books, *Customs and Cooking from the West Country* and *West Country Teas*. I hope you will enjoy making these dishes and sharing them with your family and friends.

EH

AMERICAN MEASURES

American measures are given by volume and weight using standard cups and spoons.

US Standard Measuring Spoons and Cups

1 tablespoon = 3 teaspoons = ½ fluid ounce = 14.2 ml
2 tablespoons = 1 fluid ounce = 28 ml
4 tablespoons = ¼ cup
5 tablespoons = ⅓ cup
8 tablespoons = ½ cup
10 tablespoons = ⅔ cup
12 tablespoons = ¾ cup
16 tablespoons = 2 cups = 8 fluid ounces = ½ US pint
32 tablespoons = 2 cups = 16 fluid ounces = 1 US pint.

Metric (Imperial)	American
1 teaspoon	1 teaspoon
1 tablespoon	1 tablespoon
1½ teaspoons	2 tablespoons
2 tablespoons	3 tablespoons
3 tablespoons	¼ (scant) cup
4 tablespoons	5 tablespoons
5 tablespoons	6 tablespoons
5½ tablespoons	7 tablespoons
6 tablespoons (scant ¼ pint)	½ cup
¼ pint	⅔ cup
scant ½ pint	1 cup
½ pint (10 fl oz)	1¼ cups
¾ pint (15 fl oz)	scant 2 cups
¾ pint (16 fl oz)	2 cups (1 pint)
1 pint (20 fl oz)	2½ cups

Metric (Imperial)	American
flour, plain or self-raising	
15 g (½ oz)	2 tablespoons
25 g (1 oz)	1¼ cup
100/125 g (4 oz)	1 cup
sugar, caster or granulated, brown (firmly packed)	
25 g (1 oz)	2 tablespoons
100/125 g (4 oz)	½ cup
200/225 g (8 oz)	1 cup
butter, margarine, fat	
1 oz	2 tablespoons
225 g (8 oz)	1 cup
150 g (5 oz) shredded suet	1 cup

1 cup (American) contains approximately
100/125 g (4 oz) grated cheese, 50 g (2 oz) fresh breadcrumbs,
100 g (4 oz) dried breadcrumbs,
100/125 g (4 oz) pickled beetroot, button mushrooms, shelled
peas, red/blackcurrants, 5 oz strawberries,
175 g (6 oz) raisins, currants, sultanas, chopped candied peel,
stoned dates,
225 g (8 oz) glacé cherries, 150 g (5 oz) shelled whole walnuts,
100 g (4 oz) chopped nuts,
75 g (3 oz) desiccated coconut,
225 g (8 oz) cottage cheese,
100/125 g (4 oz) curry powder,
225 g (8 oz) minced raw meat,
⅜ pint (7½ fl oz) cream.

SOUPS

WEST COUNTRY SOUP

METRIC
400 g potatoes
1 carrot
1 small leek
2 small onions
100 g bacon
¼ teaspoon marjoram
¼ teaspoon fines herbes
1 teaspoon chopped parsley
600 ml water
2 tablespoons cream
salt and black pepper

IMPERIAL
1 lb potatoes
1 carrot
1 small leek
2 small onions
4 oz bacon
¼ teaspoon marjoram
¼ teaspoon fines herbes
1 teaspoon chopped parsley
1 pint water
2 tablespoons cream
salt and black pepper

Peel and slice the potatoes. Slice the carrot. Clean and cut up the leek. Skin and slice the onions. Fry the bacon. Add the vegetables and sauté for 3 minutes. Remove from the heat and stir in the water. Add the marjoram and fines herbes. Season. Cover and simmer for 45 minutes. Purée the soup using a sieve or liquidiser. Reheat the soup. Add the cream and parsley before serving.

WINTER SOUP

METRIC	IMPERIAL
200 g potatoes	8 oz potatoes
200 g turnips	8 oz turnips
200 g carrots	8 oz carrots
200 g onions	8 oz onions
200 g celery	8 oz celery
1 litre chicken stock	2 pints chicken stock
25 g butter	1 oz butter
bouquet garni	bouquet garni
salt and black pepper	salt and black pepper

Peel and dice the potatoes, turnips and carrots. Skin and dice the onions. Place the vegetables in a pan and add the stock. Clean and cut up the celery and add to the pan. Add the bouquet garni and season. Bring to the boil. Cover and simmer for 1 hour. Remove the bouquet garni. Add the butter and heat until it has melted.

Bouquet Garni: *Use 1 bay leaf, 1 sprig of thyme and 4 peppercorns.* Tie the ingredients in a piece of muslin.

CREAM OF CHICKEN SOUP

METRIC
100 g cooked chicken meat
1 litre chicken stock
125 ml milk
25g flour
1 teaspoon lemon juice
grated nutmeg
2 tablespoons cream
salt and pepper

IMPERIAL
4 oz cooked chicken meat
2 pints chicken stock
¼ pint milk
1 oz flour
1 teaspoon lemon juice
grated nutmeg
2 tablespoons cream
salt and pepper

Blend the flour with a little of the milk. Stir in the stock. Bring to the boil, stirring to prevent lumps forming. Simmer gently for 3 minutes until the stock thickens. Cut the chicken meat into pieces and add to the stock. Season and heat gently for 15 minutes. Stir in the lemon juice and a little grated nutmeg. Remove from the heat and stir in the rest of the milk and cream. Re-heat but do not boil.

CREAM OF ONION SOUP

METRIC
1 litre milk
6 large onions
50 g butter
25 g wholemeal flour
bouquet garni
3 tablespoons cream
salt

IMPERIAL
2 pints milk
6 large onions
2 oz butter
1 oz wholemeal flour
bouquet garni
3 tablespoons cream
salt

Skin and dice the onions. Heat gently in the butter until the onions are softened but not discoloured. Add half the milk, the bouquet garni and a pinch of salt. Simmer gently for 45 minutes until the onions are cooked. Remove the bouquet garni. Sieve the soup or liquidise. Return the soup to the saucepan and check seasoning. Blend the flour with a little of the remaining milk and stir into the soup. Add the rest of the milk and bring to the boil. Heat for 2 - 3 minutes stirring while the soup thickens. Remove from the heat and stir in the cream or drop a little cream into each individual serving.

Bouquet garni: *1 bay leaf, 1 sprig of parsley, 1 sprig of thyme, 4 peppercorns.* Tie all the ingredients in a piece of muslin.

APPLE SOUP

METRIC	IMPERIAL
1 kg cooking apples	*2 lb cooking apples*
2 medium size onions	*2 medium size onions*
25 g butter	*1 oz butter*
25 g cornflour	*1 oz cornflour*
4 cloves	*4 cloves*
50 g brown sugar	*2 oz brown sugar*
600 ml water	*1 pint water*
600 ml milk	*1 pint milk*
pinch of salt	*pinch of salt*

Peel, core and slice the apples. Fry gently in the butter for 5 - 10 minutes. Skin the oinions and cut each in half. Insert a clove into each onion-half. Add the onions, sugar and liquids to the apples. Season and simmer gently for an hour. Remove the pan from the heat and take out the cloves. Sieve or liquidise the soup. Using 1 tablespoon of the soup, blend the cornflour to a thick paste. Add gradually to the soup, stirring to prevent lumps forming. Re-heat and simmer for 3 minutes to thicken.

SEA FOODS

SHRIMP CHOWDER

METRIC	IMPERIAL
1 onion	1 onion
knob of butter	knob of butter
250 ml water	½ pint water
400 g potatoes	1 lb potatoes
100 g peeled shrimps (or prawns)	4 oz peeled shrimps (or prawns)
500 ml milk	1 pint milk
50 g Cheddar cheese	2 oz Cheddar cheese
1 tablespoon chopped parsley	1 tablespoon chopped parsley
salt and pepper	salt and pepper

Skin and slice the onion. Fry lightly in the butter until soft but not discoloured. Peel and dice the potatoes. Boil the water. Remove the pan containing the onion from the heat and add the potatoes and boiling water. Season and cover. Heat gently for 15 - 20 minutes until the potatoes are cooked. Stir in the shrimps and milk. Re-heat. Grate the cheese and stir into the soup. Serve garnished with parsley.

HERRINGS IN OATMEAL

METRIC	IMPERIAL
400 g herring fillets	1 lb herring fillets
25 g oatmeal	1 oz oatmeal
1 onion	1 onion

METRIC	IMPERIAL
1 teaspoon mixed herbs	*1 teaspoon mixed herbs*
1 tablespoon vegetable oil	*1 tablespoon vegetable oil*
salt and pepper	*salt and pepper*

Skin and dice the onion. Sprinkle the herring fillets with onion, mixed herbs and half the oatmeal. Season. Roll up each fillet and secure with a cocktail stick. Place in a greased pie dish, brush with oil and sprinkle with the rest of the oatmeal. Bake in a fairly hot oven (200°C, 400°F, gas mark 6) for 20 minutes.

MACKEREL IN CIDER

METRIC	IMPERIAL
6 mackerel	*6 mackerel*
250 ml cider	*¼ pint cider*
2 tablespoons cider vinegar	*2 tablespoons cider vinegar*
4 bay leaves	*4 bay leaves*
12 peppercorns	*12 peppercorns*
¼ lemon	*¼ lemon*
1 teaspoon chopped parsley	*1 teaspoon chopped parsley*
salt	*salt*

Wash the fish and make two cuts in each side of each fish. Rub a little salt and lemon juice into the cuts. Place the fish in a wide pyrex dish. Add the cider and cider vinegar. Add the bay leaves and peppercorns. Bake in a hot oven (220°C, 425°F, gas mark 7) for 15 minutes. Remove the fish. Boil the liquid left until its volume is reduced by half and pour over the fish. Sprinkle with parsley.

SALMON MOUSSE

METRIC	IMPERIAL
200 g fresh salmon	8 oz fresh salmon
4 teaspoons gelatine	4 teaspoons gelatine
125 ml mayonnaise	¼ pint mayonnaise
4 teaspoons lemon juice	4 teaspoons lemon juice
125 ml cream	¼ pint cream
cucumber	cucumber

Clean the salmon. Simmer gently in court bouillon for 20 minutes. Remove the fish and flake when cold, taking care to remove all bones and skin. Add the mayonnaise. Whip the cream and fold into the fish mixture. Dissolve the gelatine in a little hot water. Add with the lemon juice. Pour into a fish-shaped mould. When set, turn out and garnish with slices of cucumber. Serve with brown bread and butter and green salad.

Court Bouillon: *1 litre (2 pints) water and dry white wine mixed, 1 small carrot, 1 small onion, 3 teaspoons lemon juice, 3 sprigs of parsley, 4 peppercorns, ½ bay leaf, 2 teaspoons salt.* Peel and slice the carrot. Skin and dice the onion. Place all the ingredients in an enamel saucepan and simmer gently for 20 minutes. Leave to cool. Strain before using.

CRAB SOUP

METRIC	IMPERIAL
200 g fresh cooked crab meat	8 oz fresh cooked crab meat
1 litre fish stock or water	2 pints fish stock or water
1 carrot	1 carrot
1 onion	1 onion
½ bay leaf	½ bay leaf

METRIC	IMPERIAL
1 sprig parsley	*1 sprig parsley*
25 g plain flour	*1 oz plain flour*
2 teaspoons lemon juice	*2 teaspoons lemon juice*
6 teaspoons white wine	*6 teaspoons white wine*
6 teaspoons cream	*6 teaspoons cream*
salt and pepper	*salt and pepper*

Peel and dice the carrot. Skin and slice the onion. Place the vegetables, herbs and seasoning in the fish stock and simmer for 15 minutes. Remove from the heat and strain. Mix the flour with 1 tablespoon of the stock in a small basin. Add slowly to the stock, taking care that no lumps are formed. Cook until it thickens. Heat gently for 3 minutes. Remove from the heat and stir in the lemon juice, white wine, cream and crab meat.

TROUT IN WHITE WINE

METRIC	IMPERIAL
4 trout	*4 trout*
125 ml white wine	*¼ pint white wine*
25 g butter	*1 oz butter*
salt, black pepper, fennel	*salt, black pepper, fennel*

Clean the trout and season with salt and pepper. Lightly butter a fireproof dish. Place the trout in the dish and pour over the white wine. Sprinkle with fennel leaves. Cover and bake in a moderate oven (180°C, 350°F, gas mark 4) for 25 minutes until the fish are cooked. Remove the fish. Heat the liquor left in the dish to reduce its volume slightly. Thicken with the butter and pour over the trout. Serve hot.

BAKED MACKEREL WITH RHUBARB SAUCE

METRIC	IMPERIAL
4 mackerel	4 mackerel
4 bay leaves	4 bay leaves
12 black peppercorns	12 black peppercorns
3 tablespoons cider	3 tablespoons cider
15 g butter	½ oz butter
salt	salt
The sauce	*The sauce*
200 g rhubarb	8 oz rhubarb
4 tablespoons cider	4 tablespoons cider
1 teaspoon lemon juice	1 teaspoon lemon juice
25 g brown sugar	1 oz brown sugar
¼ teaspoon grated nutmeg	¼ teaspoon grated nutmeg

Clean and fillet the fish. Place a bay leaf and 3 peppercorns on each fillet. Season with salt. Roll up each fillet and skewer with a cocktail stick. Place in an ovenproof dish, dot with butter and pour the cider over them. Cover with a lid and bake in a moderate oven (180°C, 350°F, gas mark 4) for half an hour.

The Sauce: Trim and rinse the rhubarb. Cut into small pieces. Place in a saucepan together with the cider, lemon juice, brown sugar and nutmeg. Heat gently until the rhubarb is soft. Sieve and serve hot with the mackerel.

ORCHARD HADDOCK

METRIC
500 g haddock fillets
1 onion
1 bay leaf
2 cooking apples
250 ml cider
15 g white breadcrumbs
75 g Cheddar cheese
knob of butter
salt and pepper
watercress

IMPERIAL
20 oz haddock fillets
1 onion
1 bay leaf
2 cooking apples
½ pint cider
½ oz white breadcrumbs
3 oz Cheddar cheese
knob of butter
salt and pepper
watercress

Skin and slice the onion. Peel and slice the apples. Cut up the haddock into pieces. Butter an ovenprooof dish. Place the fish, apples, onion and bay leaf in the dish. Pour the cider over the mixture. Season. Cover and cook for 25 minutes in a fairly hot oven (190°C, 375°F, gas mark 5). Remove from the oven. Grate the cheese and mix with the breadcrumbs and sprinkle over the fish. Heat under a grill for 5 minutes until browned. Serve hot, garnished with watercress.

STAR GAZY PIE

METRIC
Filling
6 herrings or pilchards or mackerel
3 eggs
1 tablespoon tarragon vinegar
2 potatoes
1 teaspoon fat
1 tablespoon breadcrumbs
2 teaspoons chopped parsley
salt and pepper
Pastry
100 g plain flour
50 g butter
4 teaspoons water
pinch of salt

IMPERIAL
Filling
6 herrings or pilchards or mackerel
3 eggs
1 tablespoon tarragon vinegar
2 potatoes
1 teaspoon fat
1 tablespoon breadcrumbs
2 teaspoons chopped parsley
salt and pepper
Pastry
4 oz plain flour
2 oz butter
4 teaspoons water
pinch of salt

Filling: Clean and bone the fish, carefully removing the heads. Grease a pie dish and sprinkle breadcrumbs over the sides and bottom of the dish. Place the fish in the dish. Season with salt and pepper and sprinkle with parsley. Lightly beat the eggs in the vinegar and pour over the fish. Peel and slice the potatoes and spread over the fish. Season.
Pastry and Pie: Sift the flour and salt together. Rub in the fat until the mixture looks like breadcrumbs. Add the water and form into a large lump. Roll out the pastry on a floured board to make a lid for the pie. Brush with milk. Make 6 slits in the pastry lid and place a fish head in each so that the heads appear to stare out of the pie. Bake in a hot oven (220°C, 425°F, gas mark 7) for 30 minutes. Serve with green salad.

MEAT

SOMERSET PORK

METRIC	IMPERIAL
1 kg fillet of pork	*2 lb fillet of pork*
40 g flour	*1 ¼ oz flour*
50 g butter	*2 oz butter*
150 g mushrooms	*6 oz mushrooms*
1 large onion	*1 large onion*
600 ml cider	*1 pint cider*
4 tablespoons cream	*4 tablespoons cream*
1 tablespoon chopped parsley	*1 tablespoon chopped parsley*
salt and pepper	*salt and pepper*

Thinly slice the pork. Place each slice between two sheets of greaseproof paper and beat with a rolling pin until all the slices are very thin. Roll the slices in half the flour and fry in the butter for 8 minutes until browned on each side. Remove the meat and keep warm. Skin and dice the onion. Peel and cut up the mushrooms if necessary. Add the onion and mushrooms to the pan. Cook gently for 5 minutes. Remove from the heat. Add the rest of the flour and work into a thick paste. Add the cider, stirring to avoid the formation of lumps. Bring to the boil and cook for 3 minutes. Return the meat to the pan. Season. Stir in the cream. Re-heat but do not boil. Serve garnished with parsley.

WEST COUNTRY STEAK

METRIC	IMPERIAL
150 g sirloin steak	*6 oz sirloin steak*
100 g butter	*4 oz butter*
2 small onions	*2 small onions*
1 tablespoon brandy	*1 tablespoon brandy*
125 ml double Devon cream	*¼ pint double Devon cream*
salt and pepper	*salt and pepper*

Season the steak and fry in the butter. When cooked, remove the meat and keep warm. Skin and slice the onions. Fry until they soften and are lightly browned. Return the steak to the pan. Pour the brandy over the meat and flame. Add the cream. Serve with French fried potatoes and green salad.

KIDNEYS IN CREAM AND SHERRY

METRIC	IMPERIAL
8 lambs' kidneys	*8 lambs' kidneys*
50 g flour	*2 oz flour*
50 g butter	*2 oz butter*
1 green pepper	*1 green pepper*
1 red pepper	*1 red pepper*
200 g long grain rice	*8 oz long grain rice*
3 tablespoons sherry	*3 tablespoons sherry*
250 ml cream	*½ pint cream*
salt and pepper	*salt and pepper*

Cut the kidneys in half and roll in the flour. Remove the pith and seeds and cut up the peppers. Fry gently in the butter for 5 minutes. Add the kidneys. Season and heat gently for 15 - 20 minutes until they are cooked through. Cook the rice in salted water for 15 - 20 minutes. Add the sherry to the cream. Remove the kidneys from the heat and add the cream/sherry mixture. Stir and re-heat but do not boil. Heap the rice in the centre of a large platter and pour the creamed kidney mixture over the rice.

ROAST LAMB WITH APPLE AND CIDER

METRIC	IMPERIAL
1 kg leg of lamb	2 lb leg of lamb
1 lemon	1 lemon
200 g cooking apples	8 oz cooking apples
15 g sugar	½ oz sugar
2 cloves	2 cloves
2 teaspoons chopped chives	2 teaspoons chopped chives
½ teaspoon ground ginger	½ teaspoon ground ginger
1 tablespoon fat	1 tablespoon fat
250 ml cider	½ pint cider
salt and pepper	salt and pepper

Bone the lamb. Rub the meat all over with the juice from the lemon. Peel, core and slice the apples. Sprinkle the fruit with sugar and add the chives and cloves. Stuff the meat with the fruit. Skewer. Rub the outside of the meat with salt, pepper and ginger. Brush with melted fat. Bake in a moderate oven (180°C, 350°F, gas mark 4) for one and a half hours. Warm the cider and baste the meat with it every 20 minutes. When the meat is cooked, decant off any excess fat. Heat the liquor left to reduce its volume by half. Serve this gravy with the meat.

HONEY ROAST DUCK

METRIC	IMPERIAL
1 duck	*1 duck*
25 g butter	*1 oz butter*
2 tablespoons honey	*2 tablespoons honey*
1 tablespoon arrowroot	*1 tablespoon arrowroot*
250 ml water or stock	*¼ pint water or stock*
Stuffing	***Stuffing***
100 g breadcrumbs	*4 oz breadcrumbs*
25 g butter	*1 oz butter*
2 large onions	*2 large onions*
2 teaspoons dried sage	*2 teaspoons dried sage*
salt and pepper	*salt and pepper*

Stuffing: Skin and chop the onions. Cook in salted water until soft. Drain off the liquid. Mix in all the other ingredients of the stuffing. Season.

Clean the duck and wipe it dry inside and out. Stuff the duck. Brush the duck with butter and honey. Roast in a moderate oven (180°C, 350°F, gas mark 4) allowing 25 minutes per 450 g (per lb). 10 minutes before cooking is complete, prick the bird's skin all over to allow excess fat to escape and raise the oven temperature to 200°C, 400°F, gas mark 6. When cooked, remove the duck. Pour off excess fat from the pan. Mix the arrowroot with the water and work into the sediment to thicken it. Gradually stir in the stock, taking care to keep the sauce free from lumps. Re-heat.

WEST COUNTRY CASSEROLE

METRIC	IMPERIAL
1 rabbit	*1 rabbit*
200 g cooked ham	*8 oz cooked ham*
2 large onions	*2 large onions*
2 carrots	*2 carrots*
25 g flour	*1 oz flour*
600 ml stock	*1 pint stock*
¼ teaspoon mixed herbs	*¼ teaspoon mixed herbs*
salt and pepper	*salt and pepper*

Skin, clean and joint the rabbit. Slice the ham. Place half the ham in the bottom of the casserole. Peel and slice the carrots. Skin and slice the onions. Cover the ham with onion. Add the rabbit joints. Then add the carrots, remaining onion, ham and herbs. Mix the flour with a little of the stock and add with the stock to the casserole. Season. If preferred, a little browning may be added. Cook in a moderate oven (180°C, 350°F, gas mark 4) for 2 hours.

SAVOURIES

DEVON ROAST

METRIC	IMPERIAL
Filling	*Filling*
200 g mutton	*8 oz mutton*
2 cooking apples	*2 cooking apples*
2 onions	*2 onions*
250 ml meat stock	*¼ pint meat stock*
salt and pepper	*salt and pepper*
Pastry	*Pastry*
100 g plain flour	*4 oz plain flour*
50 g butter	*2 oz butter*
4 teaspoons water	*4 teaspoons water*
pinch of salt	*pinch of salt*
milk	*milk*

Filling: Cut up the meat. Peel, core and slice the apples. Skin and slice the onions. Put alternate layers of meat, apples and onions in a pie dish. Season. Pour on the meat stock. Cook in a moderately hot oven (180ºC, 350ºF, gas mark 4) for 30 minutes until the meat is cooked.

Pastry and Pie: Sift the flour and salt together. Rub in the butter until the mixture looks like breadcrumbs. Add the water and form into a lump. Roll out on a floured board and cover the meat with the pastry. Brush with milk and return to the oven. Bake for 20 - 25 minutes at 200ºC, 400ºF, gas mark 6 until the pastry is cooked.

DORSET JUGGED STEAK

METRIC	IMPERIAL
1 kg stewing steak	*2 lb stewing steak*
15 g flour	*¼ oz flour*
1 onion	*1 onion*
4 cloves	*4 cloves*
125 ml port wine	*¼ pint port wine*
1 tablespoon chopped parsley	*1 tablespoon chopped parsley*
salt and pepper	*salt and pepper*
1 tablespoon redcurrant jelly	*1 tablespoon redcurrant jelly*
Sausage meat balls	***Sausage meat balls***
1 egg	*1 egg*
150 g sausage meat	*6 oz sausage meat*
25 g breadcrumbs	*1 oz breadcrumbs*

Cut up the steak and roll in the flour. Place in a casserole. Skin and slice the onion. Add the onion, cloves, parsley and port wine to the meat. Add a little water, if necessary, to cover the meat. Season. Cover and cook in a moderate oven (170°C, 325°F, gas mark 3) for two and a half hours, adding a little water if the meat tends to become dry.
Sausage meat balls: Lightly beat the egg. Mix the breadcrumbs and sausage meat with the egg. Season. Roll the mixture into small balls and dip in the flour. Add gently to boiling water and poach for 10 minutes.
Stir the redcurrant jelly into the steak mixture and then add the sausage meat balls. Cook for a further 15 minutes uncovered.

CORNISH PASTIES

METRIC	IMPERIAL
Pastry	*Pastry*
200 g plain flour	8 oz plain flour
100 g butter	4 oz butter
8 teaspoons cold water	8 teaspoons cold water
pinch of salt	pinch of salt
Filling	*Filling*
400 g chuck steak	1 lb chuck steak
150 g potatoes	6 oz potatoes
2 small onions	2 small onions
2 teaspoons mixed herbs	2 teaspoons mixed herbs
salt and pepper	salt and pepper

Pastry: Sift the flour and salt together. Rub in the butter until the mixture looks like breadcrumbs. Add the water and work into a large lump.

The pasties: Cut the steak into small pieces. Peel and dice the potatoes. Skin and chop the onions. Mix all the ingredients and season. Roll out the pastry on a floured board and cut into four rounds 20 cm (8 inches) in diameter. Divide the meat mixture between the pastry rounds. Brush the edge of each round with milk. Gather up the edge of each round of pastry to form a seam down the centre of each pasty. Flute the edge of the seam. Brush with milk and place the pasties on a greased baking sheet. Make a small hole in the top of each to allow steam to escape. Bake in a hot oven (220°C, 425°F, gas mark 7) for 15 minutes and then for 1 hour at 170°C, 325°F, gas mark 3 to cook the meat.

CORNISH PIE

METRIC	IMPERIAL
Pastry as on page 26	*Pastry as on page 26*
Filling	*Filling*
50 g lean bacon	2 oz lean bacon
1 small onion	1 small onion
4 mushrooms	4 mushrooms
1 egg	1 egg
50 g Cheddar cheese	2 oz Cheddar cheese
250 ml milk	½ pint milk
25 g butter	1 oz butter
salt and pepper	salt and pepper

Make the pastry as on page 26. Cut the pastry in half. Roll out one half and use to line a deep plate. Skin and chop the onion and mushrooms and gently fry in the butter. Chop up the bacon and add to the pan. Fry gently until cooked. Lightly beat the egg with the milk. Grate the cheese and add to the milk. Add the cooked bacon and vegetables. Mix and season. Pour into the pastry case. Roll out the rest of the pastry and cover the pie. Brush with milk. Bake in a moderate oven (190ºC, 375ºF, gas mark 5) for 30 minutes. May also be cooked open as a flan. Serve hot or cold.

HOGGAN

METRIC	IMPERIAL
Pastry	*Pastry*
400 g plain flour	8 oz plain flour
75 g dripping	3 oz dripping
water	water
Filling	*Filling*
200 g beef steak	8 oz beef steak
100 g calf's liver	4 oz calf's liver
100 g potatoes	4 oz potatoes
1 small turnip	1 small turnip
1 large onion	1 large onion
2 small carrots	2 small carrots
salt and pepper	salt and pepper
egg white	egg white
milk	milk

Pastry: Rub the dripping into the flour. Add enough water to make a firm dough. Roll out and cut into 15 cm (6 inch) rounds).

Filling: Cut up the steak and liver. Peel and dice the vegetables. Mix the meat and vegetables together. Season. Place some meat and vegetable mixture in the centre of each pastry round. Brush the edges of the pastry with egg white. Draw the edges of each round together. Brush with milk. Make a small hole in each pasty. Place on a baking tray and bake in a hot oven (220ºC, 425ºF, gas mark 7) for 50 minutes.

SAVOURY PASTY FILLINGS

PORK PASTY Use 200 g (8 oz) pork. Remove as much as fat as possible from the pork. Cut up the meat and flavour with diced onion, sage or thyme.

RABBITY PASTY Cut up 200 g (8 oz) of rabbit flesh. Season with salt, pepper and diced onions.

SQUAB PASTY Cut up 200 g (8 oz)mutton or veal. Sprinkle the meat with diced onion. Add 1 teaspoon currants and sultanas and a few slices of apple. Sprinkle with sugar and a pinch of mixed spice.

EGG AND BACON PASTY Dice 200 g (8 oz) bacon, removing as much fat as possible and mix with diced, hard boiled egg. Season with salt, pepper and a little parsley.

BACON AND POTATO PASTY Dice 150 g (6 oz) bacon, removing as much fat as possible. Peel and thinly slice 2 large potatoes. Skin and dice an onion. Mix together and season with salt and pepper.

CHICKEN PASTY Cut up 200 g (8 oz) chicken meat and mix with diced potato, carrot and onion. Season.

MACKEREL PASTY Clean and simmer 4 mackerel in salted water until cooked. Remove the skin and bones. Season with salt, pepper and parsley.

TURNIP PASTY Finely dice 200 g (8 oz) turnip. Season with salt and dot with butter.

VEGETABLE PASTY Skin and dice 2 carrots, 2 onions, 2 potatoes and 4 mushrooms. Mix and moisten with a little chicken stock.

POTATO AND BACON PIE

METRIC	IMPERIAL
200 g potatoes	8 oz potatoes
50 g Cheddar cheese	2 oz Cheddar cheese
12 g butter	¼ oz butter
2 tablespoons milk	2 tablespoons milk
1 tablespoon Devonshire cream	1 tablespoon Devonshire cream
4 slices bacon	4 slices bacon
salt	salt
parsley	parsley

Peel and boil the potatoes in salted water for 15 - 20 minutes until softened. Cut the bacon into pieces and fry crisply. Grate the cheese. Strain the potatoes and mash with the butter and milk. Stir in the cheese and cream. Place in a serving dish and cover with the bacon pieces. Garnish wth parsley.

CHEDDAR CHEESE STRAWS

METRIC	IMPERIAL
50 g Cheddar cheese	2 oz Cheddar cheese
50 g butter	2 oz butter
100 g plain flour	4 oz plain flour
¼ teaspoon plain mustard	¼ teaspoon plain mustard
1 egg	1 egg
salt and cayenne pepper	salt and cayenne pepper

Grate the cheese. Sift the flour, mustard, salt and pepper together. Rub in the butter until the mixture looks like breadcrumbs. Stir in the cheese. Mix well. Separate the egg yolk. Add to the mixture and make into a stiff dough, adding a little cold water if necessary. Wrap in greased greaseproof paper and chill for 1 hour. Roll out on a lightly floured board to a thickness of 0.75 cm (⅜ inch). Cut into 10 cm (4 inch) long strips. Place on a greased baking sheet. Lightly beat the egg white and brush the cheese straws. Bake in a fairly hot oven (190ºC, 375ºF, gas mark 5) for 20 minutes. Tie in bundles.

SOMERSET RAREBIT

METRIC
100 g Cheddar cheese
1 large onion
15 g breadcrumbs
knob of butter

IMPERIAL
4 oz Cheddar cheese
1 large onion
½ oz breadcrumbs
knob of butter

Grate the cheese. Skin and slice the onion. Lightly butter a pie dish. Place a layer of cheese in the dish and cover with a layer of onions. Repeat, ending with a layer of cheese. Cover with breadcrumbs and bake in a moderate oven (180ºC, 350ºF, gas mark 4) for 45 minutes. Serve with buttered toast.

SQUAB PIE

METRIC	IMPERIAL
Pastry	*Pastry*
100 g plain flour	4 oz plain flour
50 g butter	2 oz butter
4 teaspoons cold water	4 teaspoons cold water
pinch of salt	pinch of salt
Filling	*Filling*
1 breast of lamb	1 breast of lamb
1 kg cooking apples	2 lb cooking apples
50 g sugar	2 oz sugar
2 onions	2 onions
salt and pepper	salt and pepper

Filling: Boil the breast of lamb in salt water until it is cooked. Remove from the pan and leave the meat and stock to cool. When the meat is cold, remove the bones and as much fat as possible. Dice the meat. Peel and core the apples. Cut into slices. Skin and slice the onions. Place a layer of onion, then lamb, then apple in a pie dish. Sprinkle with sugar and season. Repeat until all the ingredients are used up. Remove the fat from the top of the cold stock. Just cover the pie ingredients with meat stock. Cover with a lid of pastry. Brush with milk and bake in a fairly hot oven (190°C, 375°F, gas mark 5) for 25 - 30 minutes.

Pastry: Sift the flour and salt together. Rub the butter into the flour until the mixture looks like breadcrumbs. Add the water and form into a a lump. Roll out on a floured board to make the lid for the pie.

HARVEST PIE

METRIC	IMPERIAL
Pastry as on page 32	*Pastry as on page 32*
Filling	*Filling*
400 g beef	*1 lb beef*
2 onions	*2 onions*
2 carrots	*2 carrots*
1 parsnip	*1 parsnip*
⅟ swede	*⅟ swede*
2 large potatoes	*2 large potatoes*
1 teaspoon mixed herbs	*1 teaspoon mixed herbs*
25 g fat	*1 oz fat*
1 tablespoon plain flour	*1 tablespoon plain flour*
salt and pepper	*salt and pepper*
milk	*milk*

Filling: Skin and slice the onions. Heat in the fat until softened. Cut up the beef and add to the pan. Turn the meat to seal in the flavour. Heat gently until the meat is well sealed. Transfer the meat and onions to a large saucepan. Peel and dice the vegetables. Add the vegetables, herbs and seasoning to the meat. Just cover with hot water and simmer gently for 30 minutes until the meat is cooked. Place the meat and vegetables in a pie dish. Work the flour into the fat and sediment in the frying pan. Add 250 ml (⅟ pint) stock from the saucepan to the frying pan, stirring to prevent lumps forming. Pour the gravy over the meat and vegetables in the pie dish. Cover with pastry as on page 32. Brush with milk and bake in a fairly hot oven (190ºC, 375ºF, gas mark 5) for 25 - 30 minutes.

CAKES AND SWEETS

APPLE CAKE

METRIC	IMPERIAL
200 g cooking apples	*8 oz cooking apples*
100 g butter	*4 oz butter*
200 g plain flour	*8 oz plain flour*
100 g sugar	*4 oz sugar*
1 egg	*1 egg*
1½ teaspoons baking powder	*1½ teaspoons baking powder*
pinch of salt	*pinch of salt*

Peel, core and cut up the apples. Sift the flour, baking powder and salt together. Rub in the butter until the mixture looks like breadcrumbs. Add the sugar to the apples and stir into the flour/fat mixture. Add the egg, lightly beaten, and mix to a firm dough. Grease a round tin. Turn the mixture into the tin and smooth out to a depth of about 2.5 cm (1 inch). Bake in a moderate oven (170ºC, 350ºF, gas mark 4) for 45 - 60 minutes. While hot, cut open and spread with butter. Serve with clotted cream.

CIDER CAKE

METRIC	IMPERIAL
100 g butter	*4 oz butter*
100 g sugar	*4 oz sugar*
200 g plain flour	*8 oz plain flour*
2 eggs	*2 eggs*
1 teaspoon bicarbonate of soda	*1 teaspoon bicarbonate of soda*

METRIC
¼ teaspoon nutmeg
125 ml cider

IMPERIAL
¼ teaspoon nutmeg
¼ pint cider

Sift the flour, bicarbonate of soda and nutmeg together. Cream the butter and sugar until light and fluffy. Beat the eggs one at a time and add to the butter mixture. Beat the cider and stir into the mixture. Fold in the flour mixture. Turn into a greased 20 cm (8 inch) cake tin and bake in a moderate oven (180ºC, 350ºF, gas mark 4) for 45 minutes.

CORNISH FAIRINGS

METRIC
100 g plain flour
1 teaspoon baking powder
1 teaspoon bicarbonate of soda
1 teaspoon ground gnger
¼ teaspoon mixed spice
pinch of salt
50 g butter
50 g caster sugar
3 tablespoons golden syrup

IMPERIAL
4 oz plain flour
1 teaspoon baking powder
1 teaspoon bicarbonate of soda
1 teaspoon ground ginger
¼ teaspoon mixed spice
pinch of salt
2 oz butter
2 oz caster sugar
3 tablespoons golden syrup

Sift the flour, baking powder, bicarbonate of soda, ground ginger, mixed spice and salt together. Rub the butter into the flour mixture until the the mixture looks like breadcrumbs. Stir in the sugar. Warm the golden syrup slightly and stir into the mixture to form a firm paste. Divide in two and form into a sausage-like roll about 5 cm (2 inches) in diameter. Cut into slices ¼ cm (¼ inch) thick. Place on a greased baking tray and bake in the centre of a fairly hot oven (200ºC, 400ºF, gas mark 6) for 8 - 10 minutes. Serve with clotted cream.

DEVONSHIRE CHOCOLATE CREAM CAKE

METRIC	IMPERIAL
100 g butter	*4 oz butter*
100 g caster sugar	*4 oz caster sugar*
100 g self raising flour	*4 oz self raising flour*
2 eggs	*2 eggs*
3 tablespoons cocoa	*3 tablespoons cocoa*
Filling	***Filling***
1 tablespoon blackcurrant jam	*1 tablespoon blackcurrant jam*
125 ml double cream	*¼ pint double cream*
Frosting	***Frosting***
50 g icing sugar	*2 oz icing sugar*
1 tablespoon cocoa	*1 tablespoon cocoa*
2 teaspoons corn oil	*2 teaspoons corn oil*
2 teaspoons milk	*2 teaspoons milk*

Cream the butter and sugar until light and fluffy. Add the eggs, one at a time, beating well. Dissolve the cocoa in 1 tablespoon warm water and beat into the mixture. Sift the flour and fold into the mixture. Line two greased 18 cm (7 inch) sponge tins with greaseproof paper. Divide the cake mixture between the two tins and bake in a fairly hot oven (190°C, 375°F, gas mark 5) for 20 minutes until the cake is firm to the touch. Turn on to a rack to cool.
Filling: Whip the cream. Brush the two flat surfaces of the cake with jam and sandwich together with cream.
Frosting: Sift the icing sugar and cocoa together. Beat in the oil and milk. Beat until the icing is smooth. Pile on top of the cake.

EXETER SANDWICH

METRIC
200 g plain flour
100 g caster sugar
100 g butter
1 egg
75 g whole almonds
raspberry jam

IMPERIAL
8 oz plain flour
4 oz caster sugar
4 oz butter
1 egg
3 oz whole almonds
raspberry jam

Rub the butter into the flour until the mixture looks like breadcrumbs. Stir in the sugar. Beat the egg and add to the mixture. Form into a ball and knead lightly. Divide in two. Roll out one half and use to line an 18 cm (7 inch) sandwich tin and spread with raspberry jam. Roll out the remaining pastry and cover the jam. Seal the edges. Skin and split the almonds. Cover the top with the nuts. Bake in the middle of a moderate oven (190ºC, 375ºF, gas mark 5) for 40 minutes.

CORNISH FRUIT LOAF

METRIC
400 g self raising flour
200 g sultanas and currants mixed
200 g demerara sugar
250 ml tea
1 egg

IMPERIAL
1 lb self raising flour
8 oz sultanas and currants mixed
8 oz demerara sugar
¼ pint tea
1 egg

Soak the fruit and sugar in the tea overnight. The following day, lightly beat the egg and add to the fruit mixture. Stir in the flour. Bake in a greased loaf tin in a fairly hot oven (190ºC, 375ºF, gas mark 5) for 30 minutes. Slice and butter.

CORNISH APPLE PIE

METRIC
Pastry
200 g plain flour
100 g butter
8 teaspoons water
pinch of salt
Filling
400 g cooking apples
75 g demerara sugar
50 g sultanas
pinch of nutmeg
pinch of cinnamon
15 g butter

IMPERIAL
Pastry
8 oz plain flour
4 oz butter
8 teaspoons water
pinch of salt
Filling
1 lb cooking apples
3 oz demerara sugar
2 oz sultanas
pinch of nutmeg
pinch of cinnamon
½ oz butter

Pastry: Rub the butter into the flour until the mixture looks like breadcrumbs. Add the water and form into a large lump.

Filling and pie: Peel, core and slice the apples. Just cover the apples with water and bring to the boil to soften the fruit. Roll out half the pastry on a floured board and line an oven-proof pie plate. Spread half the apples over the pastry. Sprinkle the sultanas, spices and sugar over the apples. Dot with butter. Add the remaining apples. Roll out the rest of the pastry and cover the pie. Brush with milk. Bake in a fairly hot oven (200°C, 400°F, gas mark 6) for 35 minutes. Serve dusted with caster sugar and topped with whipped cream.

BAKED APPLES AND CREAM

METRIC
4 firm cooking apples
8 teaspoons demerara sugar
125 ml water
15 g butter
whipped cream

IMPERIAL
4 firm cooking apples
8 teaspoons demerara sugar
¼ pint water
½ oz butter
whipped cream

Wash and core the apples. Make a thin cut in the skin around the middle of each of the apples. Place in an oven proof dish. Place two teaspoons sugar in the centre of each apple. Place a small knob of butter on top of each. Pour the water in the dish. Bake in a moderately hot oven (200°C, 400°F, gas mark 6) for 45 - 60 minutes until the apples are softened. Serve with whipped cream.

DEVON SYLLABUB

METRIC
1 lemon
100 g caster sugar
2 tablespoons brandy
2 tablespoons sherry or cider
250 ml double cream

IMPERIAL
1 lemon
4 oz caster sugar
2 tablespoons brandy
2 tablespoons sherry or cider
½ pint double cream

Extract the juice and grate the rind of the lemon. Soak the rind in the lemon juice for 3 hours. Strain. Stir in the sugar until dissolved. Add the brandy and sherry or cider to the lemon juice. Whip the cream. Add the juice to the cream and blend. Serve with sponge fingers or crushed macaroons.

APPLE PANCAKES

METRIC
Batter
100 g plain flour
250 ml milk
1 egg
pinch of salt
fat for frying
Filling
100 g breadcrumbs
75 g butter
800 g cooking apples
50 g caster sugar
⅟ lemon
1 teaspoon ground cinnamon

IMPERIAL
Batter
4 oz plain flour
⅟ pint milk
1 egg
pinch of salt
fat for frying
Filling
4 oz breadcrumbs
3 oz butter
2 lb cooking apples
2 oz caster sugar
⅟ lemon
1 teaspoon ground cinnamon

Batter: Sift the flour and salt together. Lightly beat the egg and mix into the flour. Work in half the milk. Gradually add the rest of the milk, keeping the batter smooth and free from lumps. Leave to stand in a cool place for 1 hour to soften the flour. Place a little fat in a frying pan and heat until very hot. Pour in enough batter to just thinly cover the pan, tilting the pan so that batter covers the base evenly. Turn down the heat. when one side is cooked, turn over the pancake and cook the other side. Keep the pancakes warm. (Makes about 8 pancakes.)

Filling: Peel, core and slice the apples. Squeeze the juice from the lemon. Place half the butter in a pan and fry the breadcrumbs. Turn on to kitchen paper. Add the remaining butter, apples, lemon juice, sugar and cinnamon to the pan. Cook gently until the apple is soft. Mix in the breadcrumbs. Divide the filling between the pancakes. Roll up and place in an ovenproof dish. Heat in a warm oven (170°C, 325°F, gas mark 3) for 20 minutes. Serve with whipped cream.

APPLE PUDDING

METRIC	IMPERIAL
Batter as on page 40	*Batter as on page 40*
Filling	*Filling*
400 g cooking apples	*1 lb cooking apples*
¼ lemon	*¼ lemon*
75 g caster sugar	*3 oz caster sugar*

Batter: Make the batter as on page 40.

Filling: Peel, core and slice the apples. Place in an ovenproof dish and sprinkle with juice from the lemon and caster sugar. Pour in the batter and bake in a hot oven preheated to 220°C, 425°F, gas mark 7 for 40 minutes. Serve hot with whipped cream.

STRAWBERRY PANCAKES

METRIC	IMPERIAL
Batter as on page 40	*Batter as on page 40*
Filling	*Filling*
fresh strawberries	*fresh strawberries*
caster sugar	*caster sugar*
whipped cream	*whipped cream*

Batter: Make and cook the batter as on page 40.

Filling: Wash and hull the strawberries. Place a few strawberries in the middle of each pancake and roll up. Dust lightly with caster sugar and pipe cream into the ends of each pancake.

PRESERVES

APPLE AND TOMATO CHUTNEY

METRIC
600 g apples
400 g tomatoes
125 ml vinegar
3 teaspoons salt
1 green pepper
500 g brown sugar
200 g stoned raisins
1 teaspoon mixed spice

IMPERIAL
1¼ lb apples
1 lb tomatoes
¼ pint vinegar
3 teaspoons salt
1 green pepper
1¼ lb brown sugar
8 oz stoned raisins
1 teaspoon mixed spice

Place the tomatoes in boiling water for a few minutes to remove the skins. Wash and core the apples. Cut up the tomatoes, apples, raisins and pepper. Place the spices in a muslin bag. Place all the ingredients in a saucepan and boil for one and a half hours. Remove the muslin bag. Turn the chutney into sterilized pots and close with airtight tops that are resistant to vinegar.

MARROW AND APPLE CHUTNEY

METRIC
2 kg marrow
800 g cooking apples
400 g onions
400 g brown sugar

IMPERIAL
5 lb marrow
2 lb cooking apples
1 lb onions
1 lb brown sugar

METRIC	IMPERIAL
1 litre distilled vinegar	*2 pints distilled vinegar*
15 g pickling spice	*¼ oz pickling spice*
75 g salt	*3 oz salt*

Peel the marrow, remove the seeds and cut up. Place in a bowl with the layers of marrow covered with salt and leave to stand overnight. Rinse the marrow thoroughly, drain and place in a preserving pan or large enamel saucepan. Peel, core and cut up the apples. Skin and dice the onions. Add all the ingredients to the pan. Heat until boiling then simmer gently for 2 hours, stirring occasionally, until the chutney becomes thick and there is no excess liquid. Pot in sterilized jars and seal with airtight tops that are resistant to vinegar.

APPLE AND BLACKBERRY CHUTNEY

METRIC	IMPERIAL
1 kg apples	*2 lb apples*
1 kg blackberries	*2 lb blackberries*
100 g stoned, chopped raisins	*4 oz stoned, chopped raisins*
100 g sultanas	*4 oz sultanas*
3 small onions	*3 small onions*
250 ml vinegar	*¼ pint vinegar*
200 g brown sugar	*8 oz brown sugar*
1 teaspoon salt	*1 teaspoon salt*
1 teaspoon ground ginger	*1 teaspoon ground ginger*

Wash the blackberries and place in an enamel saucepan with the vinegar. Crush and simmer for 15 minutes. Sieve. Return the blackberries to the saucepan. Peel, core and slice the apples. Skin and dice the onions. Add all the ingredients to the pan. Stir well and heat gently for 40 minutes until the mixture thickens. Pot in sterilized jars and close with airtight tops that are resistant to vinegar.

CONFECTIONERY

WEST COUNTRY FUDGE

METRIC	IMPERIAL
400 g granulated sugar	*1 lb granulated sugar*
125 ml milk	*¼ pint milk*
125 g butter	*5 oz butter*
100 g plain chocolate	*4 oz plain chocolate*
50 g honey	*2 oz honey*

Place all the ingredients in a large saucepan. Heat slowly, stirring all the time until the sugar has dissolved. Boil until the soft ball stage is reached. Remove from the heat and leave to stand for 5 minutes. Beat the mixture until it is thick and creamy. Grease an 18 cm (7 inch) square tin. Turn the fudge into the tin and mark into squares. When cold, break into pieces and store in an air-tight tin.

Soft ball stage: 113°C, 236°F. A little of the fudge forms a soft ball when dropped into cold water.

TREACLE TOFFEE

METRIC	IMPERIAL
400 g demerara sugar	*1 lb demerara sugar*
75 g butter	*3 oz butter*
100 g black treacle	*4 oz black treacle*
100 g golden syrup	*4 oz golden syrup*
125 ml water	*¼ pint water*
¼ teaspoon cream of tartar	*¼ teaspoon cream of tartar*

Place the sugar and water in a heavy saucepan and heat until the sugar has dissolved. Add the rest of the ingredients and boil until the temperature reaches the soft crack stage (143°C, 290°F). Pour into a buttered 18 cm (7 inch) square tin. Leave to cool for a few minutes and then mark into squares. When set, break into squares and store in an air-tight tin.

Soft crack stage: A drop of the toffee when added to cold water separates into threads which are hard but not brittle.

TOFFEE APPLES

METRIC	IMPERIAL
8 firm apples	*8 firm apples*
400 g demerara sugar	*1 lb demerara sugar*
50 g butter	*2 oz butter*
2 teaspoons vinegar	*2 teaspoons vinegar*
125 ml water	*¼ pint water*
1 tablespoon golden syrup	*1 tablespoon golden syrup*
8 lollipop sticks	*8 lollipop sticks*

Place all the ingredients, except the apples, in an enamel saucepan. Bring to the boil and boil rapidly for 5 minutes until the temperature reaches 143°C, 290°F, the soft crack stage. (See recipe above.) Wipe the apples and push a stick into each. Dip the apples in the mixture so that each is thickly coated with toffee. Leave to cool on greased greaseproof paper until the toffee hardens.

WINES AND BEVERAGES

CIDER

METRIC
2 kg apples
4 litres water
2 kg sugar
1½ lemons
piece bruised ginger root

IMPERIAL
4 lb apples
1 gallon water
4 lb sugar
1½ lemons
piece bruised ginger root

Crush the unpeeled apples in a wooden bowl using a wooden spoon. Boil the water and pour over the apples. Cover and leave for 2 weeks, squeezing the juice out of the apples. Strain and add the ginger. Add the sugar allowing 1 kg (2 lb) for each litre (2 pints) of juice. Squeeze the lemon juice into the liquor. Stir until the sugar has dissolved. Cover and leave to stand for 2 weeks. Remove any scum from the surface and bottle the liquor in screw-top bottles. Screw loosely and leave for 2 days before screwing tightly. Store in a cool dark place for 3 months without moving the bottles.

SCRUMPY PUNCH

METRIC	IMPERIAL
2 litres cider	4 pints cider
¼ bottle gin	¼ bottle gin
¼ bottle sherry	¼ bottle sherry
½ litre soda water	1 pint soda water
2 oranges	2 oranges
1 lemon	1 lemon
25 g sugar	1 oz sugar
4 sprigs of mint	4 sprigs of mint
soda water	soda water

Wash and slice the oranges and lemon. Mix all the ingredients together in a large bowl, adding soda water to taste. Serve chilled with ice.

CIDER FRUIT CUP

METRIC	IMPERIAL
1 litre cider	2 pints cider
500 ml ginger ale	1 pint ginger ale
500 ml tonic water	1 pint tonic water
500 ml grapefruit juice	1 pint grapefruit juice
250 ml fresh orange juice	½ pint fresh orange juice
Maraschino cherries	Maraschino cherries

Mix all the ingredients together in a large bowl. Decorate with cherries.

INDEX